# THE GREEN BAY PACKERS POCKET PRIMER

By Chuck Carlson

ADDAX
PUBLISHING
GROUP

Published by Addax Publishing Group
Copyright © 1997 by Chuck Carlson
Designed by Randy Breeden
Illustrations and Cover Design by Jerry Hirt
Cover Photos by Vernon Biever

Library of Congress Cataloging-in-Publication Data

Carlson, Chuck, 1957-
    The Green Bay Packers pocket primer / by Chuck Carlson.
        p.   cm.
    ISBN 1-886110-16-6
    1. Green Bay Packers (Football team—Miscellanea. I. Title.
GV9560.G7C365   1997
796.332'64'0977561——dc21                     97-22758
                                              CIP

Distributed to the trade by Andrews & McMeel
4520 Main Street
Kansas City, MO 64111

Printed in the United States of America
3 5 7 9 10 8 6 4 2

# Dedication

To Packer fans everywhere. Surely you know who you are by now.

# Acknowledgments

I don't know if I've ever given the proper credit to the man who has helped turn me from one of those people who always wanted to write a book to someone who now has four of these things under his belt. I owe a ton to Bob Snodgrass of Addax Publishing, who has shown an inexhaustible (almost) faith and patience in me over what has been a very long, very busy, very rewarding six months. I also have to thank him for the idea for this book, which was hatched, if I'm not mistaken, in the food court at a local mall in Green Bay. No one ever said inspiration has to come from great places.

Many thanks, again to the other great folks at Addax who always make my job easier Brad Breon, Darcie Kidson, Sharon Snodgrass and Michelle Washington.

Thanks also to my employers at *The Post-Crescent*, especially sports editor Larry Gallup, associate publisher Kevin Doyle, managing editor Bill Knutson and news editor Dan Flannery, who supplied some of the better questions for the quiz you'll read later.

I'd also like to thank Green Bay Packers president Bob Harlan, general manager Ron Wolf, coach Mike Holmgren and his players for their unending cooperation and good humor. Also, many thanks to the Packers public relations department, starting with director Lee Remmel and including Jeff Blumb, Mark Schiefelbein, Paula Martin, Aaron Popkey and Linda McCrossin. And, of course, you can't write a book on Packers fans without acknowledging the people who make it possible - the fans themselves. Without your loyalty, love and obsession toward your football team, this would be an awfully short project.

**Chuck Carlson**
**July 1997**

# Introduction

On the outside, they appear to be relatively normal.

They pay their taxes, mow their lawns when appropriate and return their video rentals on time.

There is nothing to distinguish them from anyone else except their ability to be achingly, incredibly ordinary.

But take these same people and put anything green and gold in front of them and check the reaction. Mention Brett Favre or Reggie White or Mike Holmgren or – drop and take cover on this one – Vince Lombardi and watch what happens.

Talk about the Ice Bowl or Ray Nitschke or Bart Starr and see their eyes light up. Heck, even bring up the likes of Mossy Cade, Tony Mandarich and Herman Fontenot and you'll still get a reaction.

These normal, unassuming people who live their mainstream lives in their mainstream communities with their 2.3 children and their golden retriever change when you mention the Packers. Anything about the Packers. Even from the most trivial detail.

They become the pigskin version of Pavlov's dogs, salivating and howling at the mere mention of a football team that is so much more than that to many, many, many people.

The same folks who can't find their car keys from one day to the next know why Edgar Bennett is a better runner in mud than on the turf.

The same people who can't put gasoline in their lawnmowers know the intricacies of coach Mike Holmgren's West Coast offense.

*Green Bay Packers fans take their team very seriously. For them, the season does not run from September to January, but is a year-round event.*

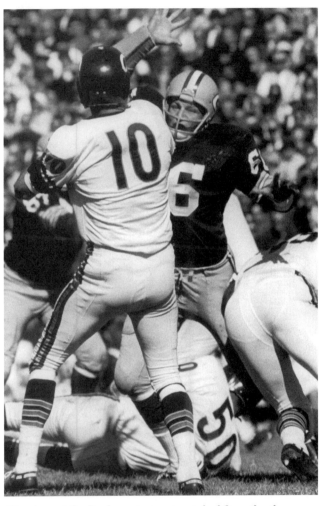

*That love of the Packers stems a great deal from the glory years of the l960s when players like Hall of Fame linebacker Ray Nitschke terrorized opposing quarterbacks. Nitschke still lives in Green Bay and remains one of the franchise's great ambassadors.*

And the same people who would turn up their noses and snort at being called a sports fan, will, without hesitation, call themselves Packers fans.

There is, after all, a huge difference.

Sports? All that is are a lot of people getting sweaty and usually being overpaid to do it. The Packers? Oh my, where do we start? There are roughly 5 million people in the state of Wisconsin and — oh — maybe 4,999,992 are Packers fans. It is a not a game to be played four months out of the year. The Packers are a way of life, a year-round obsession, a family tradition, a source of agony and pride, pain and wonder.

Packers fans. For those on the outside looking in, they are a puzzling bunch.

They are devoted to a fault. They are rabid, raucous, coarse, sometimes infuriating, always entertaining. And they are the prototype for what sports fans everywhere should, but probably never will be.

They are knowledgeable without being too smart for their own good. They can be critical without sounding shrill. And they are vitally important to the success of their football team as evidenced by the fact that the Packers have been incredibly dominant over the years on the hallowed soil of Lambeau Field.

More than that, they will without hesitation, hit the road to follow their heroes.

Defensive end Reggie White recalled one time stepping onto the field at Seattle's Kingdome and hearing more fans yelling for the Packers than the home standing Seahawks.

"I thought I'd seen it all," White said. "There were 50,000 people in the stands and 30,000 were cheering for us. That's crazy."

What's even more entertaining is watching Packers fans invade an enemy stadium and enrage the home

*Ask any Packers fan and they can tell you the history of this franchise from its inception to the players who made it great. One of them was halfback Ted Fritsch, one of dozens of players now enshrined in the Packers Hall of Fame.*

folks so much that a docile stadium suddenly becomes a snakepit.

It's like that every year in the Metrodome when the Packers and Vikings whack away at each other in their annual border war.

Without fail, at least 30,000 Packers fans trundle up north to watch the festivities and goad Vikings fans whenever possible. As a result, no matter how bad the Vikings are, the game with the Packers is always circled on the calendar and always one of the loudest, nastiest and strangest games of the season.

But while the Packers have had their problems over the years at that joint, it doesn't bother Green Bay fans, who will make the pilgrimage every season just for the sheer fun of annoying everyone in the Twin Cities.

These are people who routinely and giddily wear cheese wedges on their heads and are convinced it's normal attire. They paint their faces (and other parts of their anatomy which will not be named) green and gold and can't figure out why everyone else doesn't. They have lived and died several times over with a football team that has broken their hearts more times than the Homecoming queen. Yet they happily come back for more because this is their team and to do otherwise is not only unseemly but, quite possibly, illegal.

To their followers, of which there are millions world-wide, the Green Bay Packers are forever.

Do not make light of this. There is nothing funny or cute about Packers fans and they didn't just come out of the woodwork as soon as this team got competitive.

They have always been there, especially through the thin times of which there were countless.

And that is what separates Packers fans from those anywhere else in the country and with any other sport.

Take the lawyer from Appleton, Wis., a city 30 miles south of Green Bay, who looks you straight in the eye and says, "I'd kill for the Packers."

Take the fellow who tattooed a Packers logo on the bald spot on his head and justified it by saying, "Hell, I've got a spot up here that's kind of empty. Might as well put something up there."

Take the 31,000 people who are on the waiting list for Packers season tickets, most of whom know they won't be around by the time their name comes up.

Take the team itself, which unabashedly feeds off the frenzy produced by Packers fans and admit that when they play at Lambeau Field, they believe they cannot be beaten.

It is a scary, perplexing, heartening phenomenon and it belongs to Packers fans alone. And don't think they don't know it either.

They are only too aware these days of their place in the sports cosmos and they know that how they respond to their team will be watched by fans across the country who are interested in the right way in rooting for their team.

"There is no right way," said one Packers fan recently. "There's no handbook. It's called being loyal."

A bartender at one of the fine establishments in New Orleans' French Quarter poked his head out the door one day late in January and watched as a chanting, churning sea of green and gold rolled by.

It had been a long week for this bartender, and it was culminating on this Saturday night before Super Bowl XXXI, a game that would pit the Green Bay Packers against the New England Patriots.

He recalled how Packers fans had descended on this city a week earlier like locusts on a cornfield. He recalled how they stayed up until all hours. How they drank and ate and reveled and spent money like there was no tomorrow. How they talked about their beloved Packers as though they were some holy shrine.

And he remembered thinking how crazy and out-landish and, perhaps, a little obnoxious these people were. But he also thought about how desperately he hoped they'd come back some day.

He also thought about why his city couldn't look at their NFL team, the boring and beleaguered Saints, the same way Packers fans look at their team.

"That's the kind of support every team needs," he said. "I hope the Packers know what they have."

They do.

"Greatest fans in football," said Packers safety Eugene Robinson. "They're crazy, but they're great."

"Never seen any better," said coach Mike Holmgren.

There is no secret formula for being a Green Bay Packers fan, though it helps to come from a family where rooting for the Packers is as routine as breathing.

One Packer fan's earliest memory was sitting in the

*For Packers fans everywhere, the scoreboard in the New Orleans Superdome said everything that needed to be said.*

living room with his grandfather as he listened to Packers games on the radio. It's a rite of passage, a journey into adulthood and the pot of gold at the end of the rainbow is being able to attend a game at pro football's holiest cathedral – Lambeau Field.

Oh, and by the way, to hear Packer fans tell it, more than 3 million people were actually in attendance at the revered "Ice Bowl" game in 1967, the one in which Bart Starr snuck into the end zone with 16 seconds to play to beat the Dallas Cowboys.

Sure, it says only 40,000 were actually there, but every Packer fan claims a little piece of that one.

This is also not merely Green Bay's team. It belongs to the entire state and to much of the Midwest as well. Sure there are the Minnesota Vikings to the north, the Chicago Bears to the south and the Detroit Lions to the east, but none has the mythic nature of the Packers.

From Green Bay to Appleton to Oshkosh to Milwaukee and over to Wausau and LaCrosse and Stevens Points and up to Superior, there is nothing that binds a state together like the Packers.

But it is also a team that boasts huge followings in every state, Canada and Mexico, Europe, Asia, South America and Antarctica, as far as anyone knows.

It is a team with it's own sanctioned fan club, "America's Pack," that has 50,000 members and is growing daily.

These are people who have earned their stripes through years of torture and pain and embarrassment and redemption. It is a Greek tragedy in blaze orange, a story that is fashioned and reinvented over the years but which sounds just as good every time you hear it.

It is a story of the small-town, Green Bay, with its smoke stacks and fast food joints going up against the rest of the NFL.

The Packers should not exist in Green Bay and everyone, especially the fans, know it. So, every year, it's them against the world, a constant struggle to prove that football can still be fun and entertaining without all the corporate trappings.

The franchise is not perfect and no one would claim that it is.

It's too cold, it's too snowy and if you want night life, Chicago's just three hours away. But what Green Bay does offer is football in its most unadulterated form. It has the history most pro franchises can only dream of and the football team is idolized to the point that it stretches credibility.

Over the course of the next few pages, we'll try to identify Green Bay Packers fans, what makes them tick, how they became what they are and how you too can join the legion of followers that call themselves Green Bay Packers fans.

It is a strange, elite fraternity but, what the heck, there's always room for a few more.

# Life on the Frozen Tundra

## 1

It is model No. 1265, corresponding, naturally, to the address of Packers headquarters on Lombardi Avenue in Green Bay.

It is green and gold and looks awfully comfortable, especially considering what it's stated use is for. It has the Packers logo on it, probably gets great gas mileage and it costs a cool $3,000.

It's a casket.

As well, in the past four years, the number of newborn baby boys in Wisconsin named Brett, in honor of the Packers all-everything quarterback Brett Favre, has risen dramatically.

NEW BORNS TODAY

So, you see, people do indeed live and die with the Packers.

Check the Green Bay phone book under the business white pages.

What you'll find is nearly an entire page of listings

*It's true. Since his arrival and subsequent stardom, the number of male babies named Brett, in honor of quarterback Brett Favre, has increased in the state of Wisconsin.*

with the word "Packer" somewhere in it.

You have your Packer City International Trucks Inc. and you have your Packer Manufacturing Company. You have Packerland Auto (located on Packerland Ave., naturally) and you have Packerland Brokerage. You have Packerland Storage, Packerland Glass Products, Packer City Soft Water and the Packerland Kennel Club. There is also a country radio station with the call letters WPKR. You figure it out.

Oh, and did we mention Packerland Liquor, Packerland Chiropractic or Packer Valley Title Corp.? Nope, didn't think so.

There is Lombardi Middle School, named for the sainted head coach, and Lombardi Avenue, where the coach said during its dedication that no speeding ticket would ever be written.

And Lambeau Field rises above Lombardi Avenue like some green monolith – imposing, impressive and with so many memories, you have to swat them away like mosquitoes on a summer afternoon.

There are more than 15 books on the market about the Green Bay Packers. Everything from the glory years in the 1960s to the Bears-Packers rivalry to the yearly statistics to books on Brett Favre and Reggie White and a book from former left tackle Ken Ruettgers and even the team's long-time trainer, Dom Gentile.

You want to relive the Packers Super Bowl XXXI season? You've got three books on that alone.

And more are coming. Check your watch, there are always more coming.

Books on Vince Lombardi and another on Favre and if you wait long enough, a book on every Packer who ever set foot on Lambeau Field could well be on the market.

There have probably been more books written about the Packers, past, present and future, than have been written about the Spanish-American War.

There are two weekly publications that come out on the Packers – year round. The Packer Hall of Fame draws hundreds of thousands of visitors every year. At local banks, you can get free checking accounts by ordering checks with the big "G" on it.

Two months after the Packers Super Bowl XXXI triumph, the goalposts used in the game went on display at a sports bar in Green Bay. Thousands came to see them, even more bid to take portions home and pieces of it now reside in the Packers Hall of Fame.

And every weekend, without fail, in season and out, there are autograph signings involving Packers. It doesn't matter who and it does not matter when. Schedule the Packers No. 3 defensive end for a signing at 2 a.m. in the middle of a blizzard and the line will form a day early.

It doesn't matter. It never has.

In training camp, fans will flock over a free agent fullback from West Muleskinner State, a player with less than no chance of making the team. It matters not. He's in uniform and that's all that counts. He is a Packer. Whether he's ever seen again makes no difference because, by God, he signed my hat.

Defensive end Gabe Wilkins remembers his first encounter with Packers fans four years ago.

"My first impression was 'Whoa, these people are nuts,' " he said.

He remembered being swamped for autographs by all sorts of people – little kids, businessmen, women, old ladies, even nuns.

They were everywhere. And they wanted little more than to see a Packer up close.

"They can be real....aggressive," Wilkins said. "They expect a lot and it can be good or bad. But I know this much, it's good to have them on our side."

*The dynamic duo, as far as Packers fans are concerned, is
coach Mike Holmgren and Brett Favre.*

Yep, these people probably are crazy.

How many fans do you know that would start a petition
drive to force the Packers to give a Super Bowl ring to the
veteran left tackle Ken Ruettgers, who had retired midway through the 1996 season due to a chronic knee injury.

Gertrude Delorit of Green Bay did. She collected more than 4,000 signatures and Ruettgers got his ring. Though the Packers said he was on the list to get one anyway, you can't help but wonder if Gertrude's blitz had something to do with it.

Then there's the Ruhe family of New Berlin and the Ramlows of Big Bend, related by marriage, who could end up making the Civil War look like a Barry Manilow concert.

Since 1962, the two families split the cost of five Packers tickets for games played at Milwaukee's County Stadium.

But when the Packers pulled out of Milwaukee in 1995, the tickets, which were in the name of the Ramlows, were given to another member of the family to use. Now, they won't share and the issue is going to court.

"This is too sensitive a situation to even talk about," a member of the Ruhe family said. "The relationship is now a problem for the whole family."

Don't be surprised if this one ends up in Supreme Court and sets new legal precedent for the use of Packers tickets.

Of course, you really know if you're a Packers fan if you have a box of Lambeau turf sitting on your mantel piece.

That may be the ultimate test of Packer fanaticism because, quite frankly, to most people the idea of buying a chunk of grass for $10 a pop seems to suggest that while the lights may be on, nobody's home.

But it makes perfect sense to Packers fans, who converged — not once, or twice, but three times — to buy the torn-up turf from the NFC playoff game against San Francisco and then, later, from the NFC title game.

It went so well, raising more than $250,000 for four Green Bay charities, that one of the sales hit the road and went to Milwaukee. Part of the proceeds from that sale too went to charity and the rest went to help pay for a new, state-of-the-art field.

Ah, but these are just a few stories in the naked story. Every Packer fan who ever lived has their own.

Perhaps you didn't know that in the hour after the Packers beat the Carolina Panthers to earn their first Super Bowl trip in 29 years, long-distance phone calls from three Wisconsin cities quadrupled.

In one five-minute period prior to the game ending, Ameritech logged 300 calls into a Green Bay switching station. In the five minutes following the game, the same switching station logged 3,000 calls. And it was like that throughout the state.

"It appears Wisconsin fans were calling everywhere across the country, no doubt to brag," said a phone company official.

No doubt.

If there is a word that consistently and constantly pops up when discussing Packers fans, that word is probably "loyal."

"The one major constant is that we've been sold out on a season-ticket basis since 1964," said Lee Remmel, the Packers long-time public relations director who has been involved with the team in some capacity since 1946. "I don't think you could have a better indication than that. That's proof positive of Packers' fans loyalty."

"A true Packers fan is someone who follows them whether they win or lose," said Tom Boettcher, a fan for as long as he can remember. "There are a lot of fair-weather fans out there but that's not true of Packer fans."

"Packer fans are devoted followers," said Mary Braemer. "No matter if they win or lose, we love them."

"A Packer fan? I think it's someone who cares about them whether they win or lose," said Lyn Emenecker.

Sense a theme here?

It is that simple. The very foundation of being a Packers fan is unquestioning, unswerving loyalty to the team. Period. There is no room for doubt, for question, for uncertainty.

And that loyalty has been tested. Like some trial from the Old Testament, the Packers would come up with one more screwball way to test the faith of their flock.

From the time the Packers won Super Bowl II over the Oakland Raiders on January 14, 1968 until the time Mike Holmgren and general Ron Wolf took the stage in 1992, the Packers had four winning records. Four. That's it.

They reached the playoffs only twice, and one of those trips came thanks to that bizarre playoff tournament after the strike in 1982.

Other than that, it was a wasteland. No present and no future and just a glorious past to mock fans everywhere.

"But they always figured that the next year would be their year," said team president Bob Harlan.

It was quaint and cute and more than a little embarrassing, but what other choice did they have? It was the only game in town. So, every year, they came back with the same anticipation, the same fire, the same hope that something would change.

This is not to say that Packers fans are some mindless zealots who will cheer for their heroes even when they're playing poorly. They can be hard on the team and they can be fickle. God, can they be fickle.

Take the 1995 season-opener against the St. Louis Rams – one of those rare occasions when the Packers actually lost a game at Lambeau Field. In the first half, Brett Favre was horrible and the Packers went to the locker room trailing amidst a torrent of boos.

The year before that, in another miserable first half

*Even after so many years, Vince Lombardi remains a mythic figure among Packers fans.*

against Tampa Bay, Favre was again inundated with boos. He came out in the second half and directed a late fourth-quarter charge that pulled out the win. Afterward, defensive end Reggie White scolded the crowd for getting on Favre.

If there is anyone Packer fans identify with most, it is the quarterback. And while that can probably be said for fans of every football team, there is a particular kinship between the signal-caller and Packers fans over the years. It is also a turbulent relationship at best, going back to the halcyon days of Bart Starr.

Fans and quarterback have snapped and snarled and woofed at each other over the years simply because both expect so much from each other.

Whether it was Starr or Lynn Dickey or, God forbid, Rich Campbell or Don Majkowski or Anthony Dilweg or

*Here is Vince Lombardi and his wife Marie. Fans today continue to drive by the house the Lombardi's used to live in as though it is a shrine.*

Favre, the quarterback has always been the flash point for fans.

There was a time, perhaps you'll recall, when Don Majkowski owned this town. His blond, flowing locks, his swashbuckling air, that confident smirk that convinced you he knew more than he really did.

He was the perfect quarterback. Or at least the perfect embodiment of a quarterback.

He was the "The Majic Man" as he liked to be called and in 1989 he had the state of Wisconsin, and a fair chunk of the nation, in the palm of his hand.

You could drive anywhere in the Green Bay area or the adjoining Fox Valley and see Majkowski's image plastered up on a sign or a billboard or an advertisement. Of course, Majkowski would have endorsed spent nuclear fuel rods if it meant some extra money.

But he produced and that's all Packers fans asked.

That season, Majkowski directed the Packers to come-back win after comeback win. He'd lead improbable, impossible rallies and, to further his claim for sainthood, he even beat the hated Bears twice.

The Packers went 10-6 that season, and though they missed the playoffs, the tone had been set. The next year would be special and Packers fans were practically on the other side of themselves waiting for the 1990 season to dawn.

But, as was typical of the Packers back then, they perceived a wonderful opportunity and took system-atic, calculated steps to destroy it. And brother did they succeed.

It began when Majkowski decided that, despite hav-ing never taken his team to the playoffs (though he had thrown more career interceptions than touchdowns), it was time for a big, new contract – a contract the Packers were unwilling to pay.

The result was the dreaded HOLDOUT. And Majkowski's was a beauty, lasting until nearly the start of the regular season. Meanwhile, a likeable but over-matched fellow, Anthony Dilweg, was handed the starting job in Majkowski's absence.

Dilweg was smart, quotable and so darned cute, you just wanted to hug him every time you saw him. But there is smart and there is smart. And while Dilweg may have graduated with honors from Duke University, when it came to deciphering a two-deep zone, he was reading at a second-grade level.

But Packers fans backed the young guy nonetheless because – well – what choice did they have? And in his first start, Dilweg was magnificent, throwing for three touchdowns and earning NFC player of he week honors. And, for a briefest time, Anthony Dilweg was the king of

Wisconsin.

He was soon deposed, though, and Majkowski returned. And though resentment simmered just below the surface from most fans, they accepted him back because – well – what choice did they have? But it was clear that whatever special powers Majkowski had in 1989, they had dissipated in 1990 and the long slide began again, first to 6-10 that season and 4-12 the following year in which Blair Kiel was actually starting by the end of the season.

Oh, by the way, all the billboards with Majkowski's smiling, smarmy face on them suddenly disappeared almost overnight.

We can stop right here and say that, in the long, strong, strange history of the Green Bay Packers, that may well have been rock bottom.

Even in the dark days nearly 40 years earlier under Gene Ronzani and Lisle Blackbourne, the Packers had rarely looked this forlorn. And fans actually stayed away. Not in droves, like in other stadiums, but just enough to notice. Suddenly, there was something better to do than watch the Packers lose and it was a situation the Packers could not tolerate.

Bob Harlan, the team's president, certainly noticed and he agonized with the rest of the fans about the pathetic state of this once proud franchise.

And it was at that moment, when Harlan decided he'd had enough of really bad football, that the meter started to inch the other way.

Today, kindergartners are taught about the renaissance of the Green Bay Packers. Everyone knows the story and, like most stories, it's received a few embellishments over the years.

But the fact is that the Packers made the commitment the proper way and, of course, Green Bay fans all over

*The most famous play in Packers history was when Bart Starr snuck in from a yard out to beat the Dallas Cowboys on Dec. 31, 1967 in the celebrated "Ice Bowl." Ask any Packers fan today and they'll claim they were at the game or knew someone who attended. As a result, more than 3 million people were at Lambeau that day.*

the country watched hopefully, if tentatively, to see what would happen.

Four years later, they got their answer and the Green Bay Packers, and the fans who root for them, burst onto the national and international scene.

But it's important to remember how it all began. It was not always so that fans wore dairy products on their head and paid $75 for a players autograph.

In the beginning, you see, there was just the team. And that was enough.

Recall the early years of the Green Bay Packers, way before Paul Hornung and Fuzzy Thurston and Bart Starr and the grinning, gap-toothed demon that was Lombardi.

Way before that, in the days of leather helmets and shiny pants, the Packers, under the tutelage of the legendary Curly Lambeau, did to the rest of football what a dog does to a fire hydrant.

Since their humble beginnings in 1919, the Packers did not suffer a .500 or worse season until 1933. They didn't have another one until 1948 and, in the meantime, they won two NFL championships and added several metric tons to the legacy that would be the NFL and the Packers.

But 1948 signaled the end of an era for the Packers. The game was changing and so was the league. Suddenly, the NFL was being dominated by the big boys – New York, Chicago, Los Angeles, Detroit. Suddenly, little Green Bay seemed hopelessly out of its league.

And, by all rights, NFL football should not be in a place like Green Bay. You see, Green Bay is an anachronism. It's a city of 90,000 hardworking, mostly blue-collar souls who enjoy life to the fullest — and then some. In today's glitzy, high-powered NFL, Green Bay should have been left by the side of the road decades ago.

But it's not, and it never will be because of a singularly symbolic, but crucial, act that took place at the desperation point for this franchise.

In the 1950s, during the depths of the Packers gory years when poor attendance threatened the franchise's very existence, team officials hit on a quirky, but intriguing, idea. They decided to sell stock in the team, to make the Packers part of the community. They sold 4,634 shares at $25 a piece. They were non-voting shares and the paper itself was as valuable as a place mat as it was for charting the course of the Packers.

But it served its purpose. The stock sale was a huge hit, the team dug its way out of financial ruin and has been solvent and happy ever since. And those stock certificates, even though they never have and never will pay any dividends, are as valuable to fans today as anything from IBM or AT&T or United Airlines. And today, the Packers are once again considering selling stock to help create what amounts to a trust fund to pay, someday, for a new stadium. A share of stock today would cost $200 but Packers fans would hand over $2,000 if that's what it meant to help the team.

The Packers are a non-profit, publicly held company. In short, Packers fans own the Packers and don't think that doesn't mean the world to them.

"Because there is public ownership, there is a real sense of community," said Dr. Robert Madrigal, an assistant professor of marketing at the University of Oregon who studies the phenomenon known as sports fans. "They have a lot of committed fans and they're committed whether they win or lose. It really is a lifelong love affair these people have developed."

And over at the Sullivan-Wallen American Legion Post 11 in Green Bay, there is particular pride. After all, they are the beneficiaries, as it were, of the Green Bay Packers.

In the team's original bylaws, it was stipulated that if the franchise was ever sold or went bankrupt, all proceeds would go to Post 11 for the purpose of building a war memorial.

Try finding that in the charter of the New York Yankees or Dallas Cowboys.

The post, named after the first two Green Bay residents killed in World War I and World War II, is jealously proud of its stature, though reluctant to talk much about it. It still, however, provides an 18-man color guard for all of Lambeau Field's pregame ceremonies.

None of the veterans here want or expect that memorial

to be built. The Packers leaving Green Bay? Might as well tell Jupiter to leave the solar system. The Packers sold? Impossible, unthinkable, unconscionable.

There is a history that permeates the team, the town, the fans and everyone who comes here. And while some might argue that Packers fans live too much in the past, it was that past that sustained many of them through some very dark, very sad years.

Even team president Bob Harlan, who has worked for this team in various capacities for more than 25 years, learned again how important history is to this team.

In what he thought was a relatively tame comment about the need for the Packers to someday look for a replacement for Lambeau Field, Harlan was stunned by the response.

It was the lead story on every local TV station as well as the top story on several newspapers.

Even now, Harlan shakes his head in amazement.

"I wasn't talking about next week or next year or even five years," he said. "I just said that Lambeau Field isn't going to be around forever and we should make plans to decide how we'd pay for a new stadium. I love Lambeau Field and it has a lot of years left in it."

General manager Ron Wolf learned his lesson early, too.

After his first season, he floated the idea that the Packers might want to change their colors slightly. The idea didn't exactly thrill the masses and Wolf let the plan quickly die.

It is a special, almost mystical, relationship the Packers have with their fans. Players who had never dreamed of playing in Green Bay have come here and never want to leave. Players who saw snow only on TV have come here and thrived in the conditions. Players who thought they had played for the best organizations in football came to Green Bay and found out the truth.

And the fans have taken to each and every player, no matter where he came from or how he got there.

Andre Rison was a perfect example. Hung with the label of troublemaker after stops in Atlanta, Cleveland and Jacksonville, the desperate Packers picked Rison up off waivers in November of the Packers Super Bowl season in 1996 to help their flagging offense.

Andre Rison in Green Bay? The two images mixed about as well as whipped cream and motor oil.

But something strange happened. Rison fell in love with the Packers and with the community and the fans loved the way he played the game.

His past was his past and it didn't matter to Packers fans.

"I think I've found a home," Rison said. "I love it here."

Unfortunately for Rison, he got caught up in the numbers game and the Packers released him after the Super Bowl.

The decision stunned Rison, who had truly believed that after years of searching, he'd found the place for him, as unlikely as it seemed.

"I understand," he said. "I'll play somewhere else but I'll never play in a place like Green Bay again."

Few players do.

Perhaps the perfect testament to the Packers and their fans came from Reggie White, who stunned the football world by signing with the Packers in 1992 after one of the hottest free-agent bidding wars in history.

He was not sure why he chose Green Bay (though the four-year, $19 million contract didn't hurt) but knew only that God wanted him there.

He knew he could have gotten more money from other, more established teams. But White saw something in Green Bay and in the Packers that was too good to refuse.

So he took the chance, signed with Green Bay and became a living legend nearly overnight.

Now, White can't imagine life before the Packers. He even signed a five-year contract that will keep him a Packer until the end of his career and when he takes his inevitable spot in the Hall of Fame, he said he will go in as a Packer.

And to Packers fans everywhere, that's the way it should be.

In the final analysis, it's probably easier trying to figure out the origins of the universe than trying to decipher how Packer fans are built, what makes them run and why they do what they do when they do it – and some happily.

Is it too much nature? Too much nurture? Or simply too much Nitschke?

There are thousands of examples every year.

There's Martha's Coffee Club, which has met every weekday morning at 9 a.m. at a cafe near Lambeau Field for years simply to talk about the Packers.

There was the call put out by the Packers the week prior to their first playoff game last season after a snowfall inundated the stadium. The request was for help to shovel out the stadium and they'd pay the princely sum of $6 an hour. In the end, 150 people showed up and many others were turned away.

There are 2,000 people who will show up for a benefit basketball game between the faculty of the local middle school and the Packers. Never mind that most of the Packers never took a snap in anger last season, they are still the Packers and that's all that matters.

There's a fundraiser for a new park in town that will feature three Packers. Though most will never set foot in the park, an overflow crowd of 1,500 pay $90 a ticket.

*The new era of the Packers began in 1993 when the Packers beat out several of the NFL's marquee teams to sign hotshot free agent Reggie White.*

Then there is the anonymous tome that was faxed to a local newspaper by a Packer fan in Los Angeles. In fact, four were faxed to the paper, though each was basically the same.

Most Packers fans have probably heard this in some form or another and it is based on The Lord's Prayer, which is no big surprise since fans view the Packers as something akin to a religion anyway.

One version is called "Our Favre" (though Favre was spelled wrong in the letter, we'll make allowances) and another, slightly different, was titled "The Packers Prayer."

Bow your heads...

*Our Favre*
*Who art in Lambeau*
*Hallowed be thy arm.*
*The Bowl will come*
*It will be won*
*In New Orleans,*
*As it is in Lambeau.*
*Give us this Sunday*
*Our weekly win*
*And give us many touchdown passes*
*But do not let others pass against us.*
*Lead us not into frustration*
*But deliver us to Bourbon Street.*
*For thine is the MVP, the best in the NFC,*
*And the glory of the cheeseheads,*
*Now and forever*
*Go get em.*

We will not sit here and claim this will start a new religious movement. But its a classic example of how one idea can germinate and eventually find itself circling the globe to Packers fans everywhere.

It is simply one more example of the hold the Packers have on their fans and the lengths they'll go to support them.

It may not make sense, but no one ever said it had to.

# The Warning Signs

The dream comes again. So real, you can feel it, taste it, smell it. So clear, you can see the stubble on Brett Favre's face and here the crowd all over again. You see Andre Rison duckwalking into the end zone ahead of the pitiful New England Patriots defense. You see Reggie White wrap up Drew Bledsoe like so many Christmas packages. You see Favre prancing and cavorting around the Superdome like a kid on the final day of school.

And you see Mike Holmgren carried off the field with confetti cascading around him.

In your sleep, you smile that smile you haven't smiled since you found a quarter on the sidewalk.

You wake up from the marvelous dream feeling all soft and fuzzy. It has sustained you again, the dream of Super Bowl XXXI and at 2:54 a.m., in the teeth of mid-February, you decide to watch the replay of it again for what you estimate is the 219th time.

You pop the tape into your VCR, sit back in your chair and prepare to be overwhelmed again when you realize to your horror, astonishment and complete disbelief that your wife has taped over it with four consecutive episodes of "Dr.Quinn, Medicine Woman."

Convinced this is some cruel joke, you get another tape. This one has "How the Grinch Stole Christmas"

*This is usually a decent warning sign that you are completely and hopelessly a Packers fan.*

and that piercing, in-depth interview with Kathie Lee Gifford on it.

Frantically, you plow through every tape you own, from the family vacation in Yosemite to your cousin Elrod's wedding to the "Joys of Origami" special.

Stunned beyond speech, you stare at the snow on the television which, not surprisingly, matches the snow falling outside. And you realize, through no fault of your own, that your life is over. Finished. Done. Thanks very much, don't let the door hit you on the way out.

You consider waking the wife to ask, in a calm, reasoned tone, why in the name of David Whitehurst she would erase the most important four hours in your life.

But you know it would come out sounding like: "WFG%^$$#H(L+K!" not to mention "##$%@)UJH%$%@!$%!"

Besides, she'd look at you and say simply, "What? That? You've already watched it haven't you?"

So instead, you do the only thing you feel like doing anyway — and you weep like a three-year-old who lost his teddy bear.

It is three in the morning and you are reflecting on your shattered excuse of an existence.

Your lip quivers as you think no more Antonio Freeman, no more Doug Evans, no more Mark Chmura or Keith Jackson or Wayne Simmons. And even though you never liked him that much, no more Chris Jacke either, bless his heart.

You return to bed but you know that sleep will not come that night until you realize you can tape it again from your next-door neighbor. Or the guy next to him. Or the family down the block. Or your boss. Or your brother-in-law. Or any one of a million other people. After all, everyone taped it. Everyone has a record. Everyone. Everywhere.

You close your eyes and drift off with a smile on your face and visions of Dorsey Levens dancing in your head.

This can happen. This has happened. Wars have started over less. Nothing gets in the way of the Green Bay Packers. Even in the off-season, the team is front-page news, even when nothing is happening.

Packers fans voraciously eat up news about potential draft picks, free-agent acquisitions, coaching moves, changes at the concession stand, new turf, whatever. Anything that vaguely concerns the Packers concerns their fans. Nothing happens at Packers Central without several million of the team's closest advisors knowing about it.

True story. A Packer fan calls a local newspaper wanting to know if the rumor that Brett Favre was found drunk in an Appleton bar was true.

Not that we've heard, said the reporter.

"A cop told me he was arrested for DWI," the caller said. "He had a gun in his car too."

"Really? When was this?" asks the reporter.

"Well, I'm not sure. But I have a friend who said he talked to the cop," he responds.

"Oh yeah? What's the friend's name?"

"Is that important?"

"Just a little".

There is silence on the other end of the line.

"Never mind," he says. "I wouldn't want to get Brett in trouble anyway."

Click.

Always news. Even when there's no news.

As it turns out, Favre wasn't even in the state at the time this was supposed to have occurred.

To those legions caught in the grasp of raging Packeritis, the affliction is not that bad. Most don't even remember how or when they were infected, they just know that it runs through their veins, as natural as blood.

But if you're one of those who thinks he's immune or has passed through the epidemic unscathed, you may want to think again.

Besides, there are usually tell-tale signs that you have crossed over from a disinterested observer to a raging Packer fanatic. What follows is a list of 10 warning signs (in no particular order) that you are in danger of painting

your face the same color as when you had food poisoning on New Year's Eve. Cut them out, put them on the refrigerator and refer to them frequently. You'll thank us later.

No. 1: You camp out the night before at the Packers Oneida Street training facility just so you get a good spot for the first day of training camp.

No. 2: You aren't sure who Green Bay's starting right tackle was in 1975 but you also realize you won't be able to eat solid food until you find out.

No. 3: You go to the jeweler to get an exact replica of the Packers Super Bowl ring (zirconia, no diamonds, if you please).

No 4: You find yourself taping the Packers first preseason game even though you're watching it on TV anyway.

No. 5: You are the 21,345th name on the season-ticket waiting list and, ever so briefly, you wonder the best way of eliminating the 21,344 people in front of you.

No. 6: You get a Packers tattoo. On your forehead. Twice.

No. 7: You hire a lawyer and sue Super Bowl MVP Desmond Howard, claiming his decision to sign with the Oakland Raiders has caused severe emotional distress.

No. 8: You buy a Ford, the same car endorsed by Reggie White. The only trouble is, you work for Saturn.

No. 9: You have bought every book written about the Packers. You have picked up every piece of merchandise with the Packers name or logo on it. You have bought three acres of turf from Lambeau Field and every possible item from Super Bowl XXXI. Faced with the overflow, you come up with a simple solution and build a new house.

No. 10: You are thrilled to have Reggie Miller's autograph until you realize he plays for the Pacers, not the Packers.

These are usually pretty good tipoffs that you entered the other worldly realm of Packer obsession and that to fight it would be futile and probably a little painful.

There are no known cures at this stage though doctors at the Center for Disease Control, the Mayo Clinic and NFL Films are frantically searching for ways to turn the tide.

There are some reformed Packer fans, who battled their way back after months of deprogramming that included watching highlights of the Cincinnati Bengals and New York Jets. They now lead normal, well-adjusted lives without the Packers, though they remain in anonymity somewhere in western Kansas.

Not surprisingly, the disease was particularly rampant during the Packers remarkable Super Bowl season, when all those people who were convinced they had lives were swept up by the Packers and their exploits.

The invasion of New Orleans by giddy Green Bay fans has been well documented by now. But while thousands were systematically taking the Big Easy apart, back home, the frenzy was just as bad.

Daily, there were reports on the Packers, what the Packers were doing, what the Packers weren't doing, what the Packers considered doing.

There were reports on every aspect of the team, from

coach Mike Holmgren to the guy who puts the shoe laces in Brett Favre's shoes. But it just went to show that there was no such thing as too much information on the Packers.

And on Super Bowl Sunday, the state of Wisconsin was a mausoleum. Stores shut down. Shopping centers offered limited hours. Restaurants were empty, except those places that offered big screen viewing of the game.

There were even dozens of cars who staked out spots at the Lambeau Field parking lot for a night of tailgating, despite temperatures that hovered near zero.

Crazy? Maybe. Unexpected? Hardly.

This is what Packers fans do, especially when they've gone nearly 30 years having to watch Super Bowls between teams they could not possibly have cared less about.

But, eventually, it had to end.

Eventually, the game is over, the players have scattered to the four winds, the off-season has begun and you must find a life.

That, as Packer fans know too well, is sometimes easier said than done.

That's why, after the Super Bowl ended and the Packers incredible season came to a crashing, complete halt, local psychologists received a blizzard of phone calls from fans trying to cope with Packers aftermath.

One psychologist was most concerned by what he called "a self-fulfilling prophecy."

"Don't say, 'Because the football season is over, I will be miserable,' " he said. "Because you probably will be."

The suggestion by most of them was simply: Throw yourself into something else. Schoolwork. Reading a new novel. Volunteer work at the church.. Finding a cure for cancer.

You know, just....stuff.

*This monument, in snow and ice, to the Packers was erected just prior to the Packers NFC championship win over the Carolina Panthers.*

"People want to feel accomplishment, but they don't want to accomplish anything," said one psychologist. "They did a get a sense of accomplishment through the Packers. Now, with the Packers season over, we are forced to accomplish something on our own, which may be better than sitting around."

But make no mistake. For weeks after the season ended, a pall hung over the city, the region and the state.

It was over and there was nothing anybody could do

about it.

But Packers fans always bounce back. It is part of their nature, honed after years of crushing disappointment and promises unfulfilled.

In the end, as many Packers fans will tell you, it's useless to fight. Many have tried and many have failed. They had hoped that autumn Sundays would be spent watching the breathtaking fall splendor of Wisconsin. They had hoped they could go to the mall for some peace and quiet but knew they'd end up at the TV department at Sears watching the Packers wax the Buccaneers.

Most fans have quietly resigned themselves to the fact that, when the football season begins, their lives are no longer their own. They know they are at the whim of 45 guys dressed in green and gold who play a game most humans cannot even comprehend. It's not fair, really, that so many should rely on what so few do, but then, no one said pro football was a democracy.

And most Packers fans will tell you that they'd want to be doing nothing else. The sweet agony of Sunday watching their Packers play is just another way to reaffirm that they are alive, they are vibrant and that there is something in this world left to care about.

Then again, if any of the aforementioned symptoms get worse or you have an unshakable desire to follow Brett Favre home one night and sleep on his front porch, seek help immediately.

After all, there are limits. Even for Packers fans.

Right?

# Game 3 Day

Packers-Bears.
Packers-Lions.
Packers-Cowboys.
Packers-Vikings.

Come to think of it, Packers-Anybody.

Game Day at Lambeau Field. It is what all this nonsense is all about. It is why people root for the Packers with the zeal of some holy war and it goes a long way toward explaining to the uninitiated why this team means what it means to the populace.

Game Day is a riot of noise, color, smells and sights.

It is the cross between some Middle Eastern bazaar and a blue light special at K-Mart, with people of all sizes, shapes and backgrounds converging on the most sacred spot in Packerdom – Lambeau Field – to watch the only team any of them have ever cared about.

But let's face it. In aesthetic terms, Lambeau Field is not exactly the Sistine Chapel. It is what it was meant to

*There is nothing anywhere in sports like Game Day at Lambeau Field.*

*Game Day in the old days. This is one of the epic battles between the Packers and their ancient rivals, the Chicago Bears. This game was played in front of 4,000 folks at old Hagemeister Park. The second player from the left? That's team founder and legend Curly Lambeau.*

be, a place to watch football in as much comfort as you can muster for a franchise located uncomfortably close to the Arctic Circle.

Yet those who see it for the first time never forget it.

It's especially graphic as you drive down Lombardi Avenue (what else?) and watch as it rises over the collection of grocery stores, fast food joints and convenience stores. It dominates what there is of the Green Bay skyline and it is impossible not to stare at, even if you've driven by it a million times.

Lambeau was built for $960,000, which today would barely pay for what Reggie White uses in tape during a season. It was opened in 1957 to little fanfare and with 32,150 seats. It was not much to look at then and it's not much to look at now, even though the place now boasts nearly 61,000 seats that include enclosed club seats and luxury boxes. But while it has made its concession to modern life with the fancy new seats, it remains as it ever was – a place made of corrugated metal painted in green and gold which would probably be just as comfortable hosting a high school soccer match as the best team in the NFL.

But what the old place lacks in looks, it more than makes up for in charm and history – and there are more ghosts flying through this place than an English castle. They are everywhere and you need only to listen to hear them.

Every Packers fan has a favorite memory, a favorite game, a favorite moment that has indelibly burned itself on their brain and that makes Lambeau Field even that much more special.

Whether it was the "Ice Bowl" or the Don Majkowski pass to Sterling Sharpe that beat the Bears in 1989 or Reggie White's dominating performance over the Denver Broncos in 1994, there is something everyone can remember.

But the one thing every Packers fan remembers, and will always remember, is the image of Vince Lombardi stalking the sidelines.

What is it about that man that even today, three decades after he coached here and years after his death, continues to keep its hold on Packers fans.

Surely it is much more than the fact that he brought the Packers five NFL titles including the first two Super Bowls. It is more about how he transformed a franchise and, as an extension, a town that was going nowhere and made it believe in itself.

Even ex-players of Lombardi, several of whom still live in the Green Bay area, get misty-eyed when they talk about Lombardi, even though they admit he treated them like dogs during their playing days. That was because the coach was able to bring out the best in each and every one of them, teaching them lessons they have carried into the real world so many years later.

And the fans? Well, if there was a patron saint for the city of Green Bay and the surrounding environs, Lombardi would easily be it.

Fans not even born when Lombardi coached here speak of him in hushed, reverential terms. Old-timers recall talking to him during the off-season and remarking how cordial he really was. People still drive by the home Lombardi lived in, going slowly and somberly by as though they were looking at some shrine.

And, almost every Packers fan remembers where he or she was when the news came that Lombardi had died of cancer in 1970.

Perhaps no other coach in the history of sports has left such a mark on a community and a team the way Lombardi has with the Packers.

And it continues even today, through his son Vince Jr., who bears a stark and striking resemblance to the old coach. The son, no football genius but keenly aware of where his father's name still ranks in terms of familiarity, makes 50 to 75 motivational speeches a year, many in the state of Wisconsin, before still adoring crowds.

"I'd be a fool not to know what my father still means around here," said Vince Jr., who is 55 years old and lives in Seattle.

But all the history, all the charm, all the ghosts collide into a single grand cacophony called Game Day.

Actually, it really starts before that, back in July at training camp when fans will routinely stand the length of the fence, four or five deep, to watch practice. And they've done that for years.

It still amazed rookie center Mike Flanagan, who at the beginning of camp in 1996 asked a teammate, "Doesn't anybody in Green Bay have a job?"

There's also the tradition of kids lending their bikes to the players to ride from the practice field back to the locker room. Some players let the kids ride with them, some follow along holding their designated player's helmet, beaming as if they were holding the Holy Grail.

It's just the way it is.

For an intrasquad scrimmage midway through camp last season at Lambeau Field, 45,000 people showed up. For the Packers playoff win over the 49ers in a driving January rainstorm, there were three no-shows. For the Packers Super Bowl parade, a trip from the airport to a rally at Lambeau Field that normally takes 15 minutes encompassed three hours.

But, again, to those who have been around the Packers for years, none of this comes as a huge surprise anymore. Especially not in recent years as the Packers have methodically gotten better. Now, visiting teams would just as soon chew tinfoil than have to play at Lambeau Field.

Coach Mike Holmgren can't put a finger on why the Packers have grown so dominant at home (they went 10-0 in 1996, outscoring the opposition by an average of 32-13), he just knows that over the course of the last few seasons, they have been next to untouchable on home soil.

*This game from 1964 shows that Packers fans have long held a special place in their hearts for the Bears.*

"I think we have the best fans in football," Holmgren said. "When we play at home, they give us an extra boost. The players now believe they will win here. It's an attitude, it's a feeling. Our crowd makes it very difficult for the opposition and our guys don't believe anyone can come in here and beat us."

There is, quite simply, nothing like Game Day at Lambeau Field. You may think you know what to expect and others may have tried to alert you, but until it is experienced, it is all mere speculation.

Easily the most identifiable part of a Packers Game day, is the ritual of tailgating. It is rumored that when Jean Nicolet, the French explorer who happened to run across Green Bay in his travels some 300 years ago, he found two natives sitting next to their canoe grilling bratwurst and burgers with a keg of some native brew by their side.

Though this has not been confirmed, would anyone really doubt it? After all, it has become that much of a part of Wisconsin in general and with the Packers in particular.

Fans of other NFL teams have tried to duplicate what

transpires at Lambeau. They try awfully hard in Buffalo and Philadelphia and Kansas City and Detroit. But it is minor-league tailgating at best, compared to Green Bay. They have the spirit and the enthusiasm, but they lack the seasoning and experience to make the big-time. And any effort to try in Green Bay what they get away with in other cities would lead to the kind of humiliation that would require years of psycho-therapy.

So, a word of advice to tailgaters from other towns: Best leave it to experts unless you're under proper supervision.

It is not so much the food that makes tailgating at Lambeau Field such a religious experience. There are, you know, only so many animals who's flesh you'd like to sear on an open flame.

No, it's not the dogs or the brats or the burgers or the prime rib that make the difference. And it's not the side dishes either, though there is a couple from lovely Kaukauna, Wis. that makes a potato salad you'd donate a kidney for.

What stands Packers tailgaters apart from the rest of the rabble is the fact that in Green Bay, it's a social occasion. Whole families, entire companies get together as much as three hours before game-time to get together and talk and laugh and mingle.

They will start with omelettes and Bloody Marys and eventually graduate to steak and gin and tonics and the conversation will go down just as smoothly as any of the food.

And everyone does it.

In fact, go to any of the parking lots surrounding Lambeau Field and you'll see probably 90% of the people with grills going and tables set up. And that's in any kind of weather – from the heat of an August preseason game to the 45-below wind chills of a playoff game in

January. It doesn't matter the time or the place or the temperature. It is part of the ritual that is Green Bay Packers Game Day.

That's the difference.

But there's more to Game Day than just tailgating.

Drive down Ridge Road, which cuts just behind Lambeau Field and you'll see an odd sight. There, the neatly-kept houses with the precisely manicured lawns have been turned into parking lots. There, you'll see 75-year-old grandmothers waving a flag directing you to park right on the front lawn of a house that's just a stone's throw from the stadium. There, you'll see 12-year-olds making change for all the people who do park there (and a lot of them do for the affordable price of $7), smiling and giving them receipts.

It is capitalism run amok in lovely little Green Bay and don't be surprised, with a Super Bowl title under their belts, to see the prices skyrocket in seasons to come.

And while much has been written and said about the knee-buckling winters the Packers and their fans must endure, little has ever been said about what comes before that. If there is a more gorgeous place to watch football than Lambeau Field in the midst of a glorious autumn, I'd like to see it.

From late September until the early part of November, the area is overwhelmed with the kinds of colors you can only imagine in your wildest dreams. It is the reward, if you will, for what everyone endures after that.

And there's more. There is the unbridled frenzy of the scalping zone, an area one block from Lambeau Field that police set up to let people exert their Constitutional right to gouge folks for tickets. On a typical Game Day, a $28 end zone seat will go for $125-$150.

There is the sight, in November and December, of fans wearing their blaze orange deer-hunting gear, making Lambeau Field look like some weird orange grove. There are no half-naked cheerleaders, just a whole-some looking bunch from the nearby University of Wisconsin-

Green Bay, who valiantly try to lead cheers for a crowd that needs no help in that regard.

And then there is the latest legend, the Lambeau leap.

If there is anything keenly Green Bay and superbly Packers, it is the phenomenon known as the Lambeau Leap.

It's origins have been lost in the mists of time, shrouded in mystery and blanketed by uncertainty. It ranks up with the Shroud of Turin, the extinction of the dinosaurs and whatever happened to the guy who played Potsie on "Happy Days."

But this much is certain, the leap has become a part of Packers lore and a staple of the event that is Game Day.

The best anyone can figure, the leap started in 1993 and its author was LeRoy Butler, the ubiquitous veteran safety. It seems the Packers were slapping around the Los Angeles Raiders during a balmy December game in which the temperature almost reached 10 below. The Raiders clearly didn't want to be there and, quite frankly, the Packers were coming up with some pretty good reasons to do something else also.

Then it got interesting.

Reggie White recovered a Raiders fumble and, as he was churning downfield, he was caught from behind. He spied Butler in the corner of his eye and instinctively pitched it to him. Butler went the rest of the way for the touchdown as the crowd – through mufflers, scarves and gloves – cheered wildly.

Then, without really thinking about it, Butler did a half-gainer into the stands. The crowd went nuts again.

But The Leap didn't really catch on until the 1995 season when wide receiver Robert Brooks refined, improved and popularized the bit of pigskin gymnastics.

His first leap came when he scored a juggling touchdown against the New York Giants and, without hesitation, dove head-long into the sea of fans. They grabbed him, pounded him, spilled beer on him. It was heaven.

A tradition was born and soon Brooks was doing The Leap after every one of his touchdowns.

"You can dance and do all that other stuff in the end zone," he said. "But this, it's like you're a rock star and you're trusting the fans completely, and you dive off the stage and they throw you back on. It's the best feeling in the world. And I don't think you could do it anywhere else but here."

Following Brooks, many of the other Packers who scored did the same, with varying degrees of success. Some dove all the way and were swallowed up by the sea of green and gold humanity. Others, perhaps because of poor footing, smacked into the wall barely halfway up. But, ever helpful, fans would grab the player and yank him in and proceed to pummel him.

It continued in 1996 with a couple of wrinkles including two and three players jumping in at once. And Packer fans didn't care, they'd welcome any and all leapers. The more the merrier.

It even got to the point where fans would paint bulls-eyes or arrows, pleading with players to jump in their section when they scored.

It has grown so popular, that players around the league started leaping into the seats at their stadiums. But it looked forced and silly in those occasions. It had none of the joy and jubilation that it has at Lambeau.

As for coach Mike Holmgren, he loves the idea, too.

"I think it's great," he said. "As long as they throw them back."

Unless you've been to a Game Day at Lambeau Field on a perfect 54-degree afternoon, with the sun shining and the leaves sparkling and the fans roaring, it's almost impossible to explain.

Surely, it is like no experience anywhere else with an atmosphere a little like a college football game, a little like a birthday party and a lot like a revival meeting.

But what it is, mostly, is the gathering of 60,000 close friends with a single purpose. And that's to whip the beloved Packers home to victory. Somehow, some way.

It is that simple. And that complicated. And that's what makes it so much fun.

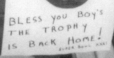

# Strangers in a Strange Land

T here is an abandoned farmhouse halfway between Green Bay and Sheboygan. Unless you're looking for it, you'll never see it even though it's just off the highway.

There it is....Over there...Next to the rusted tractor...See it?...Sure, that's it.

That's the place.

In that farmhouse, they meet every Tuesday during the football season and once a month in the off-season. You don't know them because they don't want to be known. They are nameless and faceless and they know it is best that way.

Most time, their families don't even know and, if they did, they'd be so ashamed, so disgraced. So they remain cloaked in secrecy, known only to each other and the small band of sympathizers who protect them from persecution.

*Even two New England Patriots fans, in the aftermath of the Super Bowl XXXI, had to admit the obvious.*

Who are these people who are pariahs in their own neighborhoods?

They are not Green Bay Packers fans and that is offensive enough.

There may be greater crimes in this part of the country, but most of those involve large calibre weapons.

No, there is no faster way to alienate people in Wisconsin than by walking up and proudly announcing that either A.) You don't know anything about the Packers and wouldn't know Brett Favre (you pronounce it "favor") if you fell over him or B.) You are dyed-in-the-wool, card-carrying Dallas Cowboys fan.

No one's quite sure which is more dangerous.

But these people do exist. They are all over the place, in fact, known only to each other by the secret handshake, the code word (which changes weekly) and that certain desperate look in the eye they all have.

Most of them cannot help who they are. Whether it was genetics or an accident as a youngster or something in the water, these people never developed that part in the brain that made them Packers fans. In fact, they look at those who do root for the Packers with a sort of mixture of pity, amusement and fear.

They have no idea why people wear cheese wedges on their heads. They cannot fathom why people would willingly sit in freezing temperatures on metal seats to watch two teams bloody each other into submission. They are truly perplexed about the being that is a Packers fan and they wonder, ever so briefly, why the disease never found them.

But most have grown used to how they are and they have actually come to enjoy their status as non-football fans in general and non-Packer backers in particular.

On their Sunday afternoons, while millions of others are either at the game or sitting in the front of the television watching it, these folks have what in some circles is known as "a life."

Instead of raging at Edgar Bennett for fumbling on the 4-yard-line, they are planting tulips. Instead of screeching at Antonio Freeman for dropping a touchdown pass, they are grocery shopping in a store so empty, you'd have thought a bomb scare was phoned in. Instead of railing at the Packers defense, they are taking Greek lessons or reading books or fishing or any one of a thousand things that do actually occur at the same time the Packers are playing.

These people, for obvious reasons, do not like to call attention to themselves. But we know there are a handful of them out there. They know by a look in the eye, a knowing grin when passing another follower on the street.

They know the secret handshake and they communicate through their own website: www.pleasenopackers.com.

It is a small, but loyal band and they have their principles to keep them warm.

Our story begins with Anne (not her real name, of course).

She was born and raised in Wisconsin, not far from Lambeau Field. Her parents are normal, relatively well-adjusted people until the Packers play. Then they become snorting, raging lunatics, forcing Anne to wonder if she was adopted.

Anne is no sports fan, she readily admits that. And she doesn't hate the Packers. She just doesn't have a thought about them one way or the other.

For a while she wondered if there was something wrong with her. She wondered why she didn't share her family's obsession with the green and gold.

But eventually, she came to realize she was different and that she didn't have to root for the Packers to somehow justify her life. She doesn't know exactly when that epiphany arrived, but she does know it was one of the great moments of her life.

She was, and remains, Packer free and she is exhilarated.

"I just never got into that," she said. "I never liked them. I've never been to Lambeau Field. I've never been to the Packer Hall of Fame and I have no desire to go. I also don't own anything green or gold."

Over the years, as she became comfortable with who she was, it became a game that she and her husband, who has no great love for the home team either, became awfully good at.

On the occasions when her parents would invite them over to watch the Packers on the tube, they would sometimes show up after the game has ended or, worse, they'd come on time and root for whoever the Packers were playing.

"It drives them crazy," she said with an evil laugh.

Anne continually tries to understand the obsession and devotion people have for the Packers. But she admits it's difficult to comprehend.

"There's a lot of nostalgia, I know," she said. "And people like to cling to the past. But they pour all of themselves into an overpaid team and I don't get it. These people don't have a life. Instead of treating it as a game, a sport, they take it to the ultimate extreme and they let it take over their lives."

As for the endearing qualities of Packers fans that included their loyal and unconditional love of their team, she just shakes her head.

"Outsiders think it's quaint," she said. "It's not quaint if you live here."

There are others out there as well, popping their heads into the daylight on occasion to see if the coast is clear.

Geraldo (not his real name, duh) is similar to Anne in

the respect that he doesn't understand the mechanics of a Packers fan.

"Why do they get so excited?" he asks. "I mean, it's just a game, isn't it? I remember after the Packers lost to Kansas City last season, a bunch of guys I work with didn't have a civil word to say all day. They just kept talking about the game like there was actually something they could do about it."

Geraldo, you see, is a baseball fan who has lived and died with the Chicago Cubs over the years. If anyone can understand the past torments of the Packers, it is Cubs fans, who have turned losing into an art form and disappointment into a cottage industry.

"I'm used to losing by now," he said. "So when the Cubs win, I'm happy because I never expect they will. But I always come back, every year because, eventually, they're going to win it all."

It is that part of a Packer fans dynamic that Geraldo does understand. It is the ability to forget what happened in the past, concentrate on the present and dream of the future that keeps real fans coming back. And it is the perfect description of Packers fans.

But all has not been well in the little universe that is the Packers and their fans.

In fact, the off-season following the Packers Super Bowl title, which should have been the most glorious in team history, was something less than a smooth ride.

Various missteps by your heroes, especially in the front office, had many fans wondering if their loyalties were somehow misplaced.

There was nothing major, really. Just a lot of little things that annoyed many people. Things like canceling the team's annual intrasquad scrimmage, the same one that drew 40,000 the year before. Things like raising ticket prices for the second straight year, a move that so outraged fans that exactly no one gave up their season tickets in protest.

But the biggest public relations disaster came in May when the Packers decided not to invite veteran former kicker Chris Jacke to either the team's visit to the White House or, worse, to the private party in which the team would receive its Super Bowl rings.

The firestorm of controversy was impressive, even for Packers fans.

While the team tried to explain that the ceremony was for current members and that unrestricted free agents and players no longer with the team were not invited, that didn't help.

All that did, in fact, was make it worse because that also excluded Super Bowl MVP Desmond Howard (who signed earlier with the Oakland Raiders), wide receiver Andre Rison (who was released) and linebacker Wayne Simmons (who hadn't signed with anyone at the time but re-signed with the Packers a day later).

Now Chris Jacke was never the most popular Packer anyway among fans, especially when he'd miss a 35-yard field goal in the closing seconds of a game. But the guy had eight years service with the Packers, he was three points away from being the team's all-time leading scorer and he certainly did his part to help the 1996 squad.

"I know this doesn't look good," said Packers president Bob Harlan.

He was right.

As a result, the Packers took a barrage of negative criticism from the same people who would lay down their lives for the team during the season.

"But this goes beyond loyalty to the team," said one irate woman who called into a local newspaper. "I'll still root for the Packers. I always will. But this stinks."

Many other fans felt the same way and didn't use

quite so polite verbiage. A number even said that, as of that moment, they were no longer Packer fans, though most know that until the paperwork clears, nothing is official.

But that's also part of what makes a Packer fan a Packer fan. It's the right to criticize the team when it makes a mistake – even when the team doesn't think it has.

The saga had something resembling a happy ending though. And it proved once again just how powerful a voice Green Bay fans have and how sensitive to their criticism the team has become.

A week into the brouhaha, the Packers finally relented, issuing a statement saying that all members of the 1996 Super Bowl team, whether they were still Packers or not, were welcome to the ring ceremony.

"We have always acknowledged the importance of our fans," Harlan said in a press release announcing the kind of midcourse correction worthy of a NASA moon shot. "And we have said their feelings are uppermost in our minds. The fans voiced their displeasure with our previous decision, and we listened."

As for the player who drew most of the sympathy, Chris Jacke, there was nothing but gratitude on his part.

"If it wasn't for the fans, I probably wouldn't be going," he said. "I really have to thank them."

No doubt, they responded with a raucous "You're welcome."

But that's the power Packers fans have. Can you imagine any other pro franchise changing its mind like that? And what's even more interesting is that two weeks after the firestorm, it was forgotten.

Some things, after all, take precedence.

Meanwhile, to non-Packer fans in the region, this must have looked awfully amusing. Here were the world's most loyal, forgiving fans, ripping the Packers as though they were the Dallas Cowboys or something.

But it didn't figure to last. In fact at the following minicamp just a few days later, fans were once again lined up three deep behind the fence of the team's practice facility watching the festivities.

And with the start of training camp and the realization that a new season is looming, the grumbling subsides and the focus is back on football. It always has been and it always will.

But for those who don't let the sun rise and fall on the Packers, all the turbulence meant next to nothing. After all, they have their lives nicely mapped out and thoroughly in order.

"Laundry," Anne said. "I get a lot of laundry done on the days the Packers are playing. It is the best time to get all your errands done and a good time to get all your Christmas shopping done.

If I was single, that would be a good time to go out and see if there were any single men because automatically, you'd have something in common with him."

In fact, Anne has done something of a sociological study on just who happens outside during that critical three-hour stretch when the Packers are performing.

"The only people I see out are women with young children or younger men," she said. "But never older men."

There is yet another type of person who resides in the Packer-free zone. A person who may be even more dangerous.

Mordecai (his real name – no, not really) not only isn't a Packer fan, he roots for the team that has taken its place as the Packers mortal enemy – the Dallas Cowboys.

Somewhere along the line, the Cowboys supplanted

the Chicago Bears as Green Bay's deadliest rival. It was clearly the passing of an era that probably began when Mike Ditka left the Bears and, not coincidentally, the Packers started beating up on them.

Not so with the Cowboys, who for years were the scourge of this franchise. In one four-year stretch, the Cowboys beat the Packers seven straight times, including three in the playoffs. As well, every one of those games was played at Texas Stadium.

For Packers fans, it became a quest to beat those guys.

They thought that chance might come in the 1996 NFC title game. In every Packers fan's fondest dream, the Cowboys would come to Lambeau with a Super Bowl berth on the line. The wind would be howling, the snow would be flying and the temperatures would be plummeting toward no-man's land.

And in would stroll the Cowboys, who would slip and skid and sputter while the Packers exacted rightful, delicious revenge. Of course, it didn't work out that way and the Packers still got their Super Bowl. But for many fans, it was an unfulfilled journey because it didn't include a win over Dallas.

And it's something Cowboys fans in Packer territory still love to remind them about.

"Yeah, they won the Super Bowl," Mordecai said. "But they still haven't proven they can beat the Cowboys. And they wouldn't have beaten them in the NFC title game either. The Cowboys have gotten into the Packers' heads. They have the Packers so screwed up, I don't think they could ever beat them."

There are other pockets of resistance as well. There are scatterings here and there of Tampa Bay Buccaneer fans and Bears fans and 49ers fans and Vikings fans. Unfortunately for them, the Packers have a history of beating those guys so the abuse from Packers fans is unrelenting.

"When the Packers beat the 49ers in the playoffs the last two years, I had people call me for four days giving me a hard time about it," said one Niners fan. "And they really let me have it too."

But there was also this from a Vikings fan.

"Packers fans are the greatest," he said. "They're really good-natured about things. If I hadn't been a Vikings fan since I was a kid, I'd root for the Packers."

So, make no mistake about it, they are there. Lurking. Hiding. Waiting until the sun has set before venturing outside to face the cold, cruel, Packer-dominated world. They are who they are and they make no apologies for it.

And, to their credit, Packers fans appear to be more tolerant of those who don't profess allegiance to the green and gold. They may not like them, but at least they don't beat them to a bloody pulp anymore. Now that's progress.

So the next time you're driving between Green Bay and Sheboygan, keep an eye out for that abandoned farmhouse just off the side of the road.

But enter at your own peril and, preferably, without a Brett Favre jersey.

# 5
## Does That Come in Green?

It was November, 1995 and Frank Emmert, Jr. of Superior, Wis. was in deep trouble.

He was returning home from a trip to Cleveland, where he had watched his beloved Packers whip up on the Browns, when the Cessna 172 airplane he was a passenger in developed engine trouble near Stevens Point, Wis.

As the plane was going down, Emmert knew he had to think fast to avoid what could be a disaster. In his lap, he carried one of those foam cheese wedge hats that Packers fans have come to be famous for wearing. But instead of putting it on, he used as a pillow of sorts to cushion the impact of the crash.

It worked splendidly.

And even though he suffered a serious foot injury and his right arm was cut badly, it could have – and probably should have – been a lot worse.

For his quick thinking, Emmert received national

attention, even earning a spot on the Tonight Show.

But what Emmert proved more than anything was that not only was Green Bay Packers merchandise fun, profitable and plentiful, it's pretty darned practical as well.

Where do you start when talking about the merchandising of the Green Bay Packers? What do you start with? How do you explain it?

How can a franchise in a city with 90,000 souls become so popular nationally and, for that matter, internationally?

Of course, in America today, it is not necessarily how you play on the field or the court or the diamond that matters anymore. It's how you sell in the malls, specialty shops and sports bars.

It's merchandising. It's everything from hats to t-shirts to pennants to beer mugs to flags to sweatshirts to gloves to posters to sweat pants to....well, you get the idea.

And there are few teams, in any pro sport, that are as

popular and lucrative in that field than the Packers.

Sure, some of it goes back to the golden years 30 years ago when the Packers were the NFL's dominant team with the dominant personalities. Back then, you were lucky to find a t-shirt with the Packers logo on it.

But today? Good luck trying to escape it.

You cannot turn around these days without seeing the colors or logo or designs of your favorite team. They are everywhere and anywhere, all you have to do is look.

Such is the case in our little part of the world known as Wisconsin. Whether it's the football season or not, you can see overwhelming signs of Packermania just about everywhere you look and in every part of the state.

It can be a little thing like a six-month-old baby wearing a Packers ski cap or watching perhaps 80% of kids going to school with a Packers jacket or winter coat or shorts or hat. It's adults wearing the same things during their daily journeys through life and never thinking twice about it. It's like Jay Johnson, a member of the U.S. House of Representatives (representing the Green Bay area, naturally) getting razzed by his fellow politicians about his staggering selection of Packers ties.

It is just part of the wardrobe around here and you could probably count on one hand the number of families who don't have something with the Packers logo on it.

Let some statistics, courtesy of NFL Properties (the league's licensing division), tell the story.

First and foremost, the Packers appearance in Super Bowl XXXI set a sales record for Super Bowl merchandise, netting a cool $130 million.

But there's more.

The Super Bowl triumph also resulted in sales of more than 650,000 of those locker room hats worn by the players (at $25 a pop) in the locker room after the game. That set a record held by the Chicago Bulls, who sold of their locker room hats the year before.

"Those things went faster than the 'Tickle Me Elmo' doll," said one local seller of Packers paraphernalia. "Everyone and their mother is a Packer fan."

But there's more.

More than 950,000 official Super Bowl game programs were sold, shattering the mark of 700,000 set in 1986 when the Chicago Bears beat the Patriots.

But there's more.

NFL Films churned out the "instant" highlight film of the Packers Super Bowl triumph and a staggering 65,000 were sold in the first five days. That, by the way, was a record as well.

But there's more.

Even QVC, the television sales show, had to supplement its phone line capacity to handle the demand for Packers goodies.

In 1992, the Packers were the 20th-most popular team in the NFL, in terms of the sale of their stuff. After the end of the 1995 season, they had climbed to fifth. And after last season, the Packers were second and closing fast on – you guessed it – the Dallas Cowboys.

"The Packers have had a tremendous surge in sales, not only through Green Bay, Milwaukee and all of Wisconsin, but nationally as well," said Chris Widmaier, the NFL's director of corporate communications. "To be No. 2 overall, would mean every single person in Wisconsin would have to buy eight to 10 pieces of merchandise."

Which, come to think of it, sounds about right.

But what it really means is that the Packers are hot

nationwide. They have captured a country's imagination and, more important, they have held it.

In the past year, the Packers have doubled their amount of merchandise sales. And the green and gold stuff people buy go along way toward keeping the Packers franchise in the green.

But Packers fans don't really care about market shares and how big a percentage they account for. All they know is that they love anything with "Packers" or the classic "G" on it.

There isn't enough time or paper or bytes in a computer to catalogue everything the Packers have on the market. And there's even less time to talk about why people buy the stuff without even thinking twice about it.

They do it because they want to. That's answer enough.

But, for the sake of argument, let's chronicle some of the stuff the Packers sell and some of the stuff Packers fans buy with giddy abandon.

Well, for starters, it should be understood that there are 43 styles of caps sold with the Packers emblem on it. That's right, 43.

They take different styles. They have different look. Some are leather. The color schemes vary. But they all have the same thing in common and we all know what that is, don't we?

Packer jerseys can be found on just about every kid in Northeastern Wisconsin. But it's not just the No. 4 of Brett Favre or the No. 92 of Reggie White that you'd expect. It's everyone.

From wide receiver Robert Brooks to lineman Bob Kuberski, who played not a snap during ther 1996 season. It's Pro Bowl safety LeRoy Butler and center Frank Winters and halfback Edgar Bennett and everyone in between.

It is also tight end Mark Chmura, who, sensing he could be on the threshold of something after a Pro Bowl season in 1995, incorporated himself. He also began his own line of women's swimwear with his familiar No. 89 stitched into a...ahem...strategic spot.

It is Favre, who last September became a registered trademark to dissuade counterfeiters from using his name, face and autograph for dastardly purposes.

It is coach Mike Holmgren, who is fighting the urge to do endorsements despite a flood of offers that have come his way.

And there are Packers fans – long-suffering, faithful as the night is long, giddy like children on Christmas Eve – waiting to scarf up anything and everything that is Packers.

"I knew the numbers would be high," said another store manager after a recent barrage. "Anything that has Packers on it was really hot."

We could spend all day on just the items that run toward the mainstream. But what about the other stuff? What about the items you wouldn't normally expect to be embossed with a Packers logo? The stuff you decide you must have despite the ridicule that may come your way? The stuff that sets you apart from being just a Packers fan and evolving into something more.

How about a Green Bay Packers mouse pad? You know, the one with Vince Lombardi's picture on it and a motivational saying from the surly one on it.

We've got them. Trust me.

A Packers toilet seat? A wind sock? A shower curtain? Dog collars? Christmas tree ornament? Golf head covers? Earrings? Clocks? Suspenders (or a belt if you prefer)? And enough styles of sweat shirts that will keep you clothed through the millennium?

It's all there. Somewhere. All you have to do is open your eyes (there are also Packers sun glasses, by the way).

In fact, there are more than 1,000 Packer products officially licensed by the NFL and if the Packers don't license them, chances are, you don't need them.

And here's some stuff that will give you food for thought – literally.

Perhaps you've considered green and gold loaves of bread or hamburger buns? How about green and gold shrimp platters? Or maybe football-shaped summer sausage? Or green and gold cakes, cookies and ice cream.

They've got it all and if you can put food coloring in it, it can be eaten. And Packers fans, real Packers fans, never think twice about imbibing. Even the shrimp.

It may not make a lot of sense to those from the outside looking in. Heck, it probably doesn't even make that much sense to Packers themselves. But they all know that it's the best way they have of showing support to the team.

Even other state events such as Milwaukee Brewers games or University of Wisconsin football or basketball, the predominant colors will be green and gold. There is no disrespect meant to the other sports, it is, quite simply, part of the ensemble that any Packer lover knows about from the time he's old enough to get out of his green and gold diaper.

In fact, if you were to watch the consummate Packer fan in his preparation for that day's game, it would be almost like watching an astronaut prepare for a space walk.

Depending on the weather (oh, let's say it's around 30 and sunny for kickoff), he would begin with his Packers wool socks and boxer shorts (no, seriously). He would put on his Packers sweat shirt and sweat pants, paint his

*Royal Boehlke of Random Lake, Wis. earns a special place in*
*the Packers fans hall of fame with this creation unveiled at*
*the 1996 NFC title game. Boehlke concocted an eight-foot tall*
*head dress that featured the head and shoulders of an eight-*
*point buck he'd shot. Above that, flew a Packers flag. The*
*whole thing weighted nearly 40 pounds, but he wore it most of*
*the game to the delight of his fellow fans. "I really didn't think*
*I'd get that much attention," he said.*

face the appropriate colors, strap on his official Packers winter coat and gloves and, perhaps, add something else just to get people talking.

Earning a spot in the Packers fans hall of fame last season was Royal Boehlke of Random Lake, Wis., who went to the NFC title game and showed his support in a unique way – even for a Packers fan.

Despite the 20-below wind chill, Boehlke wore an eight-foot tall head dress that included a full shoulder of an eight-point buck he'd shot. And above the buck, flew a Packers flag.

"Sometimes the wind really whipped me," said Boehlke, who estimated the whole package weighed nearly 40 pounds. "I really didn't think I'd get that much attention. I couldn't go 30 steps without someone stopping me. I had 100 people high-five me."

And why not? These people know class when they see it.

Drive around Northeast Wisconsin (which loosely encompasses everything from a little north of Green Bay all the way south to Fond du lac and even over to Lake Michigan if you so desire) and you'll see monuments to the Packers of all kinds.

From a life-sized ice-sculpture of Brett Favre to Packer logos cut into corn fields to a cheese head left on a statue in New Orleans, fans have never been shy about showing their allegiance. Whether it's a simple display of loyalty, like a single bumper sticker or one of those car flags that seem to be handed out by the DMV, to entire vehicles painted in Packer colors, the goal is the same.

"I don't pretend to understand why Packers fans are the way they are," said one man who was a devote 49ers fan. "I've never understood and I've lived here all my life. But I will say this, I admire their passion."

*Tony Canadeo had a distinctive nickname he earned in his years playing college football.*

# From Johnny Blood to Fuzzy ... A Quiz for Real Fans

For the first five chapters, the goal has been to bring you along slowly. There was no throwing you in the deep end and expecting you to swim. Nope, that would have been unfair.

This was a slow, methodical indoctrination into the world of Green Bay Packers fanaticism – who they are, what they are, where they come from, how they got here and whether you have what it takes to join the ever-growing legions.

What follows are 25 questions to test the synapses of even the most ardent, passionate, maniacal Packers fan. After all, rooting for the team is one thing, knowing every detail about the franchise is quite another. As a result, this will be no stroll through the mall, gang.

So strap on your green and gold thinking caps, take the test, see where you stand and then test your friends. Oh my, the fun you will have. Each question will be given a point value depending on its difficulty. Add up the score afterward and prepare to be amazed. Or ill.

QUESTION ONE (5 points)

The Packers 1991 draft is generally considered to be one of the worst in team history and may well have been the final nail in the coffin for coach Lindy Infante and player development director Tom Braatz. Who was the

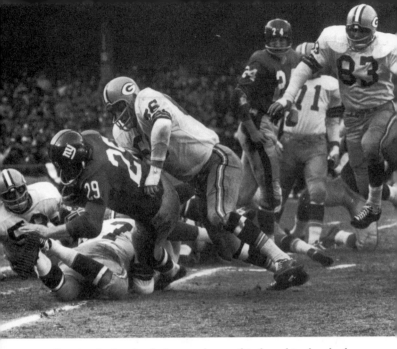

*Despite the boatload of great players this franchise has had, Ray Nitschke is one of the few this happened to.*

left-footed punter taken in the fifth round of that draft, a player Braatz called "a steal?"

QUESTION TWO (15 points)

Desmond Howard set an NFL record with the most punt return yardage in a season. Who held the Packers record before that, how many yards was it and in what year did he do it?

QUESTION THREE (5.5 points)

This is easy. Most hardened fans know that Beloit handed the Packers their first-ever professional loss in 1919. But how many Packers touchdowns were disallowed because of penalties in that game?

## QUESTION FOUR (8.2 points)

From what movie did Hall of Fame halfback Johnny "Blood" McNally take his nickname? Extra credit if you can name the star.

## QUESTION FIVE (25 points)

In his senior season at the University of Alabama in 1955, future Packers quarterback Bart Starr was second in the nation in punting. Who was first? And for extra credit, name the school he attended.

## QUESTION SIX (4.7 points)

Who did Brett Favre complete his first pass to as a Packer and how many yards did it gain?

## QUESTION SEVEN (6 points)

What team did Vince Lombardi defeat to earn his first victory as Green Bay's head coach and what was the score?

## QUESTION EIGHT (13.4 points)

When William "Refrigerator" Perry of the Chicago Bears scored a touchdown against the Packers on Monday Night Football in 1985 and vaulted into the national spotlight, what Packers linebacker did he flatten on his way into the end zone?

## QUESTION NINE (10 points)

In 1971, the legendary Packers linebacker Ray Nitschke lost his starting job. Who replaced him and what school did he go to?

## QUESTION 10 (9 points)

Who was the ex-Packer with tried, and failed, to tackle Desmond Howard on his 92-yard kickoff return for a touchdown in the Super Bowl?

## QUESTION 11 (2 points)

How many Packers are in the Pro Football Hall of Fame?

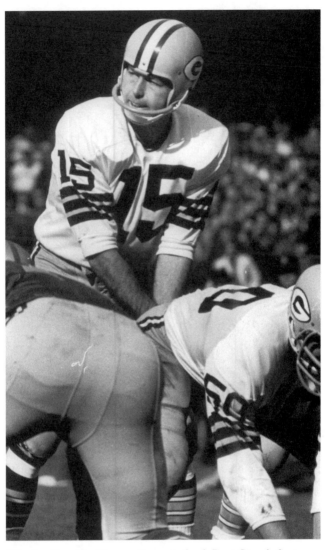

*The familiar No. 15 wasn't quarterback Bart Starr's first number as a Packer.*

## QUESTION 12 (14.7 points)

What was the nickname for Hall of Fame halfback Tony Canadeo?

## QUESTION 13 (28.4 points)

How many Packers have had their numbers retired? For extra credit name the players. And to really amaze and mystify your friends, what were the numbers?

## QUESTION 14 (8 points)

In the 1994 NFC divisional playoffs, the Packers defense put on a record-setting performance against the Detroit Lions. What did the defense do and who did it do it to?

## QUESTION 15 (14 points)

Defensive end Ezra Johnson was probably best known by Packers fans for being a fearsome pass rusher and for munching a hot dog on the sidelines during a game that enraged the coaching staff. What college did Johnson go to?

## QUESTION 16 (19 points)

When he came to the Packers as their top draft pick in 1988, a gregarious Sterling Sharpe said he would always be available to talk to the media. But by midseason, he'd stopped and never talked to the state media again. What was his reason?

## QUESTION 17 (13.3 points)

How many 1,000-yard rushers have the Packers had in their history and who were they?

## QUESTION 18 (18.2 points)

Who was the first African-American player in Packers history and what year did he join the team?

## QUESTION 19 (13 points)

Who was Green Bay's first-ever draft choice? What position did he play? What school did he attend?

*Wide receiver Don Hutson still holds a number of Packer receiving records.*

## QUESTION 20 (5 points)

What fate befell Dan Devine during his first game as Packers coach in 1971?

## QUESTION 21 (9 points)

Who was Green Bay's leading passer in 1991?

## QUESTION 22 (30 points)

What was Bart Starr's first number as a Packer?

## QUESTION 23 (15.6 points)

How many team records does Hall of Fame receiver Don Hutson still hold, more than 50 years after he retired?

## QUESTION 24 (1 point)

Just so everybody gets one answer correct: Who scored Green Bay's first touchdown in Super XXXI?

## QUESTION 25 (15 points)

At the current rate, how many years will it take for the last person on the Packers season ticket waiting list to finally get tickets?

Answers: 1. Jeff Fite. He was cut in training camp. 2. Billy Grimes, 555 yards in 1950. 3. Three. 4. "Blood and Sand" starring Rudolph Valentino. 5. Zeke Bratkowski of Georgia, who would go on to serve as Starr's backup for years. 6. He completed the pass to himself when the ball was batted back at him. He lost five yards. 7. The Chicago Bears, by a score of 9-6. 8. George Cumby. 9. The University of Minnesota's Jim Carter. 10. Mike Bartrum, who was traded to the Patriots despite an impressive training camp with Green Bay. 11. 24, if you count players who spent part of their career in Green Bay. Otherwise, it's 19. 12. "The Grey Ghost of Gonzaga" 13. Only four numbers have been retired: Tony Canadeo (3), Don Hutson (14), Bart Starr (15) and Ray Nitschke (66). 14. The defense held the Lions dan-

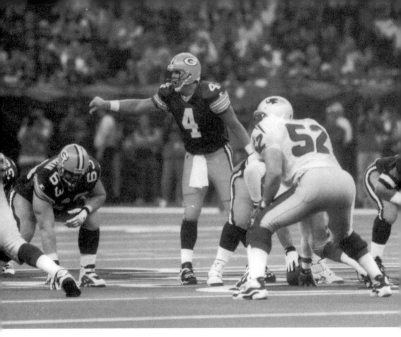

*Brett Favre's first completion as a Packer went to an unlikely source.*

gerous running back Barry Sanders to an NFL playoff record minus one yard rushing on 13 carries in a 16-12 Packers win. 15. Morris Brown College. 16. He said he did not appreciate being criticized for the number of passes he dropped as a rookie. 17. Five. Tony Canadeo, Jim Taylor, John Brockington, Terdell Middleton and Edgar Bennett. 18. End Bob Mann was traded from the Lions in 1950. 19. Guard Russ Letlow was drafted in 1936 out of San Francisco. 20. He broke his leg against the New York Giants during a sideline collision. 21. Mike Tomczak. 22. No. 42. 23. He still owns 17 team records including most passes caught in a game (14), most career touchdown receptions (99), most consecutive seasons leading team in receiving (10) and most career 200-yard games (4). 24. Wide receiver Andre Rison, on a

54-yard pass from Brett Favre. 25. Don't ask, you don't really want to know the answer.

## SCORING SCALE

0-75: You are no Packer fan. In fact, it may be necessary to check you for a pulse. To you, the Packers are one of those Sunday annoyances that get in the way of watching all-star figure skating on TV. To you, Brett Favre was a character in "Gone With the Wind" and Lambeau Field is an airport.

76-175: Not bad. You seem to have your priorities in some sort of order. You enjoy watching the Packers but you rarely consider suicide when they lose. You know the team's history, you still have Ken Bowman's autograph somewhere and you know the deal for John Hadl was a huge mistake but you're not quite sure why.

176-250: You are entering the point of no return. You have several different Packer wardrobes, each corresponding to how the team played that week. You attend training camp religiously and you grade the players on how they perform each day. You are the only one on your block who tapes the game on two VCRs in case something happens to one of them and you are on a first-name basis with everyone at the Packers Pro Shop. Your life is still your own – but just barely.

251 and above: Uh-oh. Not only did you smoke this quiz, you ridicule it for not being more difficult. Quite simply, the Green Bay Packers are your reason for existing. You know the final score of every game your heroes have ever played and, if prompted, you will recite the play-by-play of Super Bowl XXXI, complete with down, distance and crowd noise. And when you finally shake off this mortal coil, it is your fondest wish — no, your demand — that you be cremated and your ashes spread over Lambeau Field, or Mike Holmgren's front lawn, whichever is more convenient.

*This is the kind of weather Packers fans thrive in.*

# The Once and Future Fans

The date is January 27, 1997. It is bitterly cold and snow is falling in Green Bay (what else?) when the Packers charter jet arrives back in town.

The team clambers onto buses and prepares for a celebration parade that will conclude with a ceremony at Lambeau Field, maybe five miles down the road.

What the team doesn't know is that 300,000 people await on the parade route. And they are everywhere. In store fronts. On sidewalks. On rooftops. On porches. They are dressed in all manner of Packer garb. They are half-naked, with only green and gold paint, and the memories of a remarkable season, to keep them warm.

They are old and young. They have taken off from work. They are playing hookey from school.

They are everywhere. And their sole purpose is to honor the Green Bay Packers.

*A common sight on Game Day is the elusive quest for tickets. Most go away unhappy especially if it's an important game. Come to think of it, most of them are important.*

Because of the sheer mass of humanity, the parade slows to a crawl and the ceremony at a soldout Lambeau Field is delayed nearly three hours.

But no one at Lambeau leaves. Not a soul.

Finally, the team arrives. And though cranky, tired and maybe a little annoyed, it all melts away when the crescendo of cheers begins. It swells and grows and the weary faces of the players break into smiles of appreciation and amazement.

"You came out in the freezing cold for this?" says wide receiver Don Beebe in genuine awe. "You guys are the greatest."

Sometimes, it's easy for the players to forget what their fans meant to them. Packers fans can be overbearing at times. They can be outlandish and loutish and embarrassing and little ridiculous on occasion. But they are as devoted and loving as a parent with a newborn.

And they are everywhere.

From small towns in the Northwoods of Wisconsin to Milwaukee and Eau Claire and Madison. From the East Coast to the Southwest to the West Coast to Europe and Asia, Packers fans are everywhere.

They are joined by a kind of kinship that goes beyond what happens on a football field or on a scoreboard. They have known for years what players in the program sometimes never figure out – the Packers are forever. They are as constant as the sunrise, as certain as a shadow and as important as oxygen.

They are like no fans anywhere else and they know it too.

Hopefully, this little guide has helped bring the phenomenon known as Green Bay Packers fans a little more into focus. Then again, maybe that's not possible.

Maybe trying to explain Packers fans and how they tick is like trying to explain Santa Claus or why it rains every time you wash your car.

Some things, in the long run, don't need explanations. Some things just need to be enjoyed and appreciated for what they are.

Maybe a thousand years from now, when archaeologists dig up the remains of a once-great civilization, they will find the rusted hulk of Lambeau Field, the fossil imprint of a cheesehead hat and torn remnants of a sweatshirt with a large white "G" on it.

The archaeologists will nod their heads and knowingly and lovingly return the artifacts to where they found them.

"Packers fans," one will say.

It is all that needs to be said.

*Reggie White, perhaps the most popular current Packer,
salutes the fans for all they have done, and will continue to do,
for the team.*

# Photo Credits

Vernon and Jim Biever 8, 20, 24, 25, 28, 34, 52, 82, 84

Chris Dennis 4, 14, 16, 36, 38, 44, 46, 56, 58, 70, 72, 78, 86, 88, 90, 92, 94

Illustrations by Jerry Hirt